NEW TESTAMENT BELIEVERS
&
THE LAW

#2 The One New Man Series

by
Paul & Nuala O'Higgins

© 2003 by Paul & Nuala O'Higgins

ISBN 0-944795-04-8

All rights reserved. Permission to copy (with acknowledgement) for study purposes granted. No part of this publication may be reproduced for commercial resale without permission of the publisher.

Published by Reconciliation Outreach Inc

P.O. Box 2778, Stuart, Florida 34995

Printed in the United States of America

CONTENTS

Introduction		5
Chapter 1	An Ancient Controversy	9
Chapter 2	Does the New Testament Correct the Hebrew Scriptures?	13
Chapter 3	Discharged From the Law	29
Chapter 4	Maintaining Jewish Identity	37
Chapter 5	Replacement Theology	47
Chapter 6	Jesus Brings a New Era	51
Chapter 7	Objections & Refutations	61
Chapter 8	Conclusion	75
Appendix	Let the Scriptures Speak!	79

INTRODUCTION

This book is addressed to all believers who love the Jewish people and who are aware of their debt to them. It is also addressed to Jewish believers in Messiah,

The re-emergence of Messianic Judaism since the reestablishment of the State of Israel in 1948 is one of the most important developments for the future of Israel and for the future of Christianity.

Paralleling this great movement is another movement among ' Gentile' believers in Jesus who recognize God's end-time plan for Israel and the Jewish people. They are repenting of historical anti Semitism, anti Semitic traditions and replacement theology (the teaching that the church has replaced Israel)

Messianic Jews (Jews who have come to personal faith in Jesus) are in fact the oldest kind of Christians. All of the first apostles and the first 3000 believers in Jesus as well as the writers of the New Testament (with the possible exception of Luke) were Jews. Through the centuries since the fall of the Temple and the scattering of Israel there have been thousands of Jewish people who have embraced the message and work of Jesus. Sadly, in the past, inclusion in the church has resulted in their losing their Jewish identity.

Since the restoration of Israel, Jewish believers in Jesus are rightfully anxious to retain their Jewish identity. They do not wish to be assimilated, but wish to continue to identify with the irrevocable call and destiny God has for them as a people.

The questions now arise:

- How can a Jewish believer in Jesus be faithful to Jesus without compromising his Jewishness?

- How can the Jewish believer be faithful to his Jewishness without compromising his New Testament freedom?

- How can Christian supporters of Israel who wish to dissociate with anti Semitic traditions best show their solidarity with the Jewish people without losing their evangelical liberty?

- And how can Christians recognize their Jewish roots and keep their ability to adapt the gospel of the kingdom of God to every culture ?

> *How can a Jewish believer in Jesus be faithful to Jesus without compromising his Jewishness? And how can he be faithful to his Jewishness without compromising his New Testament freedom?*

This book is written to throw light on some of these issues. It is the second in the four part "One New Man" series, which, we hope, will equip God's people with a perspective which embraces both the uniqueness of Israel and the centrality of Jesus.

Traditionally Jesus has been presented as the ***dividing*** factor between the Jewish people and Gentile believers. Our aim is to present the Person, work and message of Jesus (as Paul did) as the factor which *unites* believing Gentiles and believing Jews into one New Man. *"For he is our peace, who has made us both one, and has broken down the dividing wall of hostility, by abolishing in his flesh the law of commandments and ordinances, that he might create in himself **one new man** in place of the two, so making peace and might reconcile us both to God in one body through the cross, thereby bringing the hostility to an end. (Eph 2:14-16)*

This One New Man is the people of God from every nation, grafted into the Olive Tree of Israel and receiving the blessings of Abraham through Jesus.

We dedicate this book to Jewish people who are still uncertain about the messianic claims of Jesus and to Christians who are still uncertain about the uniqueness of Israel today. Our prayer for all of us is that our eyes may opened to see more clearly *the "mystery of the gospel"*[1] and *the mystery of Israel.*

---

[1] Ephesians 6:19   Romans 16:25

1

AN ANCIENT CONTROVERSY

During the early years of the Church the issue of keeping the Law caused heated debate among the apostles. This issue was settled at the Council of Jerusalem at which it was clearly stated that gentile believers in Jesus should not be required to keep the Law.

"For it seemed good to the Holy Spirit and to us to lay upon you no greater burden than these things necessary: that you abstain from things offered to idols, from blood, from things strangled, and from sexual immorality!" (Acts 15:28-29)

The apostle Paul develops this theme throughout his writings and especially in his letters to the Galatians, the Romans and to the Colossians. Not only were the gentile believers of the early church not REQUIRED to keep the Law of Moses, but they were WARNED AGAINST going under the Law at the expense of 'severing' their relationship with the Messiah:

"For as many as are under the works of the law are under a curse. For it is written, "Cursed is EVERYONE who does not continue in ALL THINGS, which are written in the book of the law to do them!" (Galatians 3:10)

He says that those who would put believers in the Messiah "under the law" are turning away from the Messiah and creating 'another gospel'!

"But even if we or an angel from heaven preach any other gospel to you than what we preach to you, let him be accursed!" (Galatians 1:6, 8, 9)

These striking statements of Paul create some problems for Jewish believers and seekers. Is Paul saying that the New Testament is opposed to the Hebrew Scriptures? Is he saying that believers in Jesus are discharged from the moral law?

Believers Are Not Antinomian

The question now arises if we are NOT justified (reconciled to God) by the Law, but by faith in the atoning work of God in the Messiah, are we then under no law? Are we without law and therefore lawless?

It is true that some believers have drawn this conclusion and live lives free not only from the Law of Moses, but lives devoid of godliness and without discipline.

In reaction to this antinomian position (the position that says that believers in Jesus are discharged from *all* law), some have developed new sets of laws and church traditions to keep believers from slipping into fleshly living. Others react to the antinomian position by teaching that though believers are justified by faith, they should still keep the Law of Moses as a matter of obedience and to deter the flesh and maintain an upright, moral and spiritual walk. As commendable and seemingly holy as these ideas may seem to be to the believer striving to live a godly life, such practices have no power to curb the flesh. (The believer can only overcome the flesh by being filled continuously with the Holy Spirit, and by 'reckoning' his old man dead with Christ.)

"Therefore, if you died with Christ from the basic principles of the world, why as though you lived in the world, do you subject yourselves to regulations, 'Do not touch, do not taste, do not handle ... These things indeed have an appearance of wisdom in self-imposed religion, and false humility, and neglect of the body, BUT ARE OF NO VALUE against the indulgence of the flesh." (Colossians 3: 20-23)

"Likewise you also, reckon yourselves to be dead indeed to sin, but alive to God in Christ Jesus our Lord" (Rom.: 6-11)

These rules and principles of legalism are of no more value in restraining Jewish 'flesh' than they are in restraining gentile 'flesh'

2

DOES THE NEW TESTAMENT CORRECT THE HEBREW SCRIPTURES?

The New Testament does not negate, correct or oppose the Hebrew Scriptures, rather it fulfills them. Jesus said: *"Think not I am come to destroy the law and the prophets I am not come to destroy but to fulfil."* (Matthew 5:17)

The teaching that we are not justified by the law but by faith in the atoning sacrifice of Jesus, the Messiah is of course entirely consistent with the teaching of the Hebrew Bible. God foresaw that no one could be justified through the law because of the weakness of the flesh. And so He provided the system of sacrifices (in The Tabernacle and later The Temple) to provide atonement for the guilt of the people. God accepted these Temple sacrifices by which the worshipper acknowledged his guilt and then transferred his guilt to an innocent animal as a means of Atonement. .

Isaiah foresaw the day that the Lord God would lay on an innocent sinless human being the sins of all. *"All we like sheep have gone astray; we have turned every one to his own way; and the LORD has laid on him the iniquity of us all."* (Isaiah 53:6) Jesus of course was that innocent one who bore the sins of the world and all who believe in Him are cleansed from their sins by faith. Two things were involved in the Temple sacrifices, the acknowledgment of personal guilt and the acceptance of the substituionary death of the innocent animal. Similarly in the New Testament two things are involved

- acknowledgment that we cannot be justified by works of the law because each one of us has sin
- and acknowledgment of the sufficiency of God's perfect Sacrifice for all in the blood of Jesus.

So Paul's teaching on justification and atonement is not a correction of the Hebrew scriptures but an explanation of them.

The book of Leviticus clearly shows that no one can stand in God's presence on the ground of having perfectly kept the Law. All men stand in need of Atonement. This need of Atonement is one of the dominant messages of the Torah. It is amplified by the historical fulfillment of the events foreshadowed by temple sacrifices - the death and resurrection of Jesus. Paul plainly explains that all men stand in need of the benefits of the atoning sacrifice of Jesus since none of us can be justified by our attempts at keeping the law. The teaching of Paul then is not contrary to the Law and the prophets

In spite of the impression given by many Christian teachers Paul's teaching of justification though faith is *not new* to the New Testament. It was taught throughout the Bible. Christians often mistakenly teach that the Old Testament teaches justification by works while the New Testament teaches justification by faith.[2] Paul points out that Abraham and the Patriarchs were righteous by faith before the Law was instituted. The true teaching of the Hebrew Scriptures is that righteousness is by grace through faith. Righteousness was never by the Law. It was added to restrain unrighteousness not to establish righteousness.

The Temple sacrifices were an anticipation or "type" of the Perfect Sacrifice of God's own Son for the sin of the world. The Sinai commandments anticipated the day when we would be upright from the inside out and would have God's love and righteousness imparted in our hearts. (Jer 31:31)

The Permanence Of The Law

The precepts of the Law testify against all of us that we are guilty and we need either to die for our

---

[2] Early Reformation writers projected on to the Old Testament their argument with Medieval Catholicism and taught that the Old Testament taught righteousness through works and the New Testament righteousness through faith. Paul's teaching is that righteousness by faith has always been the teaching of the whole Bible, but that religious teachers had lost sight of this reality.

sins or have a substitute take our punishment. The Law cannot make us righteous but it shows us our need of the righteousness that can only come from God.

Through the Law my sin is exposed and my need of atonement is revealed. Through the Law the hypocrisy of the one who thinks that he does not need to come to God for mercy and receive the benefits of the blood of Jesus is torn away. Through the Law the testimony of sin and guilt is shown to hang over all men.

The Law is not removed or abandoned it stands as an indictment against the entire world.

- It is an indictment against the moral reprobate and tells him that fierce judgement awaits him unless he repents.
- It is an indictment against the respectable 'good' person because it reveals to him that he too is a sinner and therefore guilty of the whole Law and considered guilty in the sight of God.
- It is an indictment against the religious self-righteous person who tries to stand before

God on the grounds of his own morality. It exposes that his religiosity is not sufficient to remove his guilt.

The Law brings knowledge of sin and testifies against all of us that there is no hope for us except through the Mercy of God made available through the blood of Jesus.

We cannot put it better than the remarkable Jewish pastor, Richard Wurmbrand: *"It is amazing for a soul to discover that God gave a law to be observed but that its observance is not taken into account as a means of salvation. Then why was the Law given? What good are moral standards? They were not given because God had the illusion we could conform our lives to them. God knows that we are a degenerate race and that there is nothing good in our carnal nature.*

The law serves another purpose: to show us our sins. Man is confronted with a moral law that is just and good. His mind while acknowledging that there is the truth confesses at the same time that he does not live according to this law. And no matter how hard he tries, he realizes he does not reach the ideal.

This is how he discovers he is a lost sinner. This is the great purpose of the Law. It teaches us what sin is and shows us how wrong we are, just as a mirror reveals how filthy we are and what needs cleansing. But just as a mirror does not and cannot wash us but only reveals our condition so the law cannot correct us but only shows what great sinners we are. The purpose of the Law is to make you know your sin, so that you will begin to pray with the psalmist, 'Do not enter into judgement against Your servant, for in Your sight no one is righteous.' (Psalm 143:2)."

We cannot effectively preach God's grace to unbelievers until God's Law is first preached and our corrupt nature is exposed. We cannot recognize their need for God's forgiveness until we first recognize we have failed to meet the standards' of God's Law. No one can appreciate the greatness of God's grace in Christ unless the Law exposes his guilt and reveals its wretched and eternal consequences. Nor can anyone appreciate what it is to be redeemed from the curse of the Law through Christ until they first recognize the reality and depth of the curse of the Law. .

The Law has a *permanent* work even in the dispensation of greater grace. It so exposes our sin that we are compelled to look up to Him who alone can help us. When this *permanent ministry of the Law* is ignored, the amazing grace of God made available in Messiah Jesus cannot be fully understood.

Can The Law Perfect Us?

All believers in the gospel agree that no one is JUSTIFIED by the Law, but the question arises: can we be SANCTIFIED, OR PERFECTED by the Law? The Letter to the Hebrews answers this question for us by saying that 'the law made NOTHING PERFECT' (Hebrews 7:19) i.e. NO believer (Jew or gentile) will come to perfection (maturity) by using the Law as a guide to his behavior. Paul says it is our custodian until the Messiah comes who puts His love in our hearts. It restrained us from evil until the sin principle (the heart of stone) is removed from within us. *"So that the law was our **custodian** until Christ came, that we might be justified by faith. But now that faith has come, we are no longer under a **custodian**."* (Galatians 3:24-25)

Jesus Brought A New Covenant & A New Law

The Letter to the Hebrews (which was written mainly to Jewish believers in Jesus) tells us that *'when the priesthood is changed, there is of necessity also A CHANGE IN THE LAW'.* (Hebrews 7:12) It explains that the ministry of Jesus mediates a 'better covenant' than the Sinaiatic covenant. This better covenant is the NEW COVENANT "with the HOUSE OF ISRAEL & THE HOUSE OF JUDAH" which was foretold by the prophets (e.g. Jeremiah Chapter 31, Ezekiel 36, and Isaiah 53).

By inaugurating the New Covenant *'He has made the first obsolete"*(Hebrews 8:13) The old Law has been made obsolete for those who enter and live in the New Covenant. Every believer in Jesus will agree that He brought 'a change in the priesthood'. His priesthood is not a Levitical priesthood but a kingly priesthood, replacing and fulfilling the Levitical priesthood. The change of the priesthood of necessity brings with it a CHANGE OF THE LAW according to the writer of Hebrews.

In changing the priesthood Jesus brought in a New Covenant and a New Law. He did not leave us lawless. He left us a new law that we should love one another as He has loved us. (John 13:34)

This new commandment cannot be fulfilled by the carnal nature, but only by the life and presence of the Holy Spirit in us, who sheds the love of God abroad in our hearts so that we are filled with love for God and for one another. (Romans 5:1-5)

The prophet Jeremiah foretold the day when God would make a New Covenant with the HOUSE OF JUDAH AND THE HOUSE OF ISRAEL (not merely with the gentiles). In this New Covenant God promised to write His law on the peoples' hearts. (See Jeremiah 31) This law that He writes on the hearts of believers through the Messiah Jesus is not the Mosaic Law, but the law of love. He does not write the Torah in our hearts by the Holy Spirit but He sheds the love of God abroad in our hearts by the Holy Spirit.

Paul writes: *"Therefore being justified by faith, we have peace with God through our Lord Jesus Christ: by whom also we have access by faith into this grace wherein we stand, and rejoice in hope of the glory of God. And not only so, but we glory in tribulations also: knowing that tribulation worketh patience; and patience, experience; and experience, hope: and hope maketh not ashamed; because the love of God is shed abroad in our hearts by the Holy Ghost which is given unto us."* (Romans 5:1-5)

When we put our faith in the substituionary death of Jesus for us we stand acquitted of our sins before God, Christ having taken the punishment we deserved. We are then reconciled with God, the

> *The New Testament fulfills the purpose and the aim of the law, which was to produce believers who loved God and love their fellow man.*

barrier of guilt and sin is removed, and the Holy Spirit pours God's love into our heart. . This love enables us to love God, love ourselves and love others and so fulfills the righteousness, which the Law aspired to. And so we fulfill the purpose of the Law to produce people walking in fellowship with God and in love with Him and with one another.

At Sinai God spoke words that are memorized by nearly every faithful Jew: *"Hear O Israel the Lord our God the Lord is one! You shall love the Lord your God with all your heart with all your soul and with all your strength...and these words shall be in your heart."* (Deuteronomy 6:4-5) Jesus quoted this when asked which was the greatest commandment and added that this commandment together with the commandment to love your neighbor as yourself (Leviticus 19:18) support all the Law and the Prophets. (Matthew 22:37-40). It is this love that is poured into our hearts by the Holy Spirit when we are reconciled to God through the Atoning Sacrifice:

- Love *for* God *from* God love

- *for* ourselves *from* God and
- love *for* one another *from* God.

The Sinai Covenant, though its standards were excellent was powerless to make men righteous and so brought with it a testimony of condemnation and guilt. In Jesus this righteousness is not only upheld but it is produced and exceeded..

'But now the righteousness of God APART FROM THE LAW is revealed, BEING WITNESSED TO BY THE LAW AND THE PROPHETS, even the righteousness of God which is through faith in Jesus Christ to all and on all who believe!' (Rom. 3:21-22)

Does Our New Relationship With The Law Contradict The Hebrew Scriptures

In saying that the old law is becoming obsolete he is not saying that the Torah is becoming obsolete. This would clearly be a contradiction of the scripture, which declares that the word of God endures forever. But he is saying that the *ordinances* of the law were given to restrain evil until the time when the New Heart was to be implanted within us. Then the restraints against the evil within us erected by the law begin to be obsolete as the Spirit of God establishes righteousness in our hearts. *"But we know that the law is good, if a man use it lawfully; knowing this, that the law is not made for a righteous man, but for the lawless and disobedient, for the ungodly and for sinners, for unholy and profane, for murderers of fathers and murderers of mothers, for manslayers."* (1 Tim 1:9) When the Lord gives us a clean heart and puts His Spirit in us then we receive an inner righteousness and it becomes unnecessary for us to be restrained by external law.

This also establishes the teaching of the Hebrew Scriptures. The prophets looked to the day when God's righteousness would be placed *within* all believers, His law written in our hearts and the heart of stone (the selfish sinful nature) would be replaced with a heart of flesh (a soft righteous heart). The restraining regulations of the Sinai Law were never intended to be a permanent system.

Moses himself foretold: *"The LORD your God will raise up for you a prophet like me from among you, from your brethren--him you shall heed."*(Deut 18:15) This prophet who brought in a deeper ethic than the ethic of Mount Sinai is of course Messiah Jesus

Should Jewish Believers in Jesus Keep The Law?

We have seen that the New Testament clearly teaches that the gentile believer is not required to keep the Law. In fact he is admonished NOT to do so at the risk of 'severing' himself from Christ. But what about the Jewish believer in Jesus? Perhaps the Council of Jerusalem (See Acts chapter 15) and the rest of the New Testament only dispenses *gentiles* from the requirement to keep the Torah Laws. Perhaps the requirement of the Law is still binding on the Jewish believer in Jesus? Should the Jewish believer be REQUIRED to keep the Law to demonstrate his faithfulness to his call and to his tradition? ABSOLUTELY NOT! Paul dearly states that ALL (i.e. both all Jews as well as all gentiles) who rely on works of the Law are under a curse. (Galatians 3:10). He passionately warns his readers not to go back to 'weak and beggarly elements:'

*"But now after you have known God, or rather are known by God, how is it **that you turn again** to the weak and beggarly elements, to which you desire again to be in bondage? You observe days and months and seasons and years. I am afraid for you, lest I have labored for you in vain!" (Gal. 4:9-11)*

Apparently some of the Jewish believers in the Galatian churches were reverting to the Law, and Paul was in anguish lest this undo his apostolic work among them. (It is sometimes argued that the Galatian church was a purely gentile church, but this is evidently not the case as he could not have accused gentiles of turning 'AGAIN' to the elemental principles of the Torah. Gentiles were never under these laws in the first place. This passage has to be seen as a warning to the Jewish believer in Jesus not to be entangled AGAIN in keeping the Law.)

3

DISCHARGED FROM THE LAW

In Romans Paul makes the point even more clearly (and it is universally acknowledged that the congregation in Rome consisted of Jews as well as gentiles). Here he says that through the death of Jesus *"we are DISCHARGED FROM THE LAW, DEAD TO THAT WHICH HELD US CAPTIVE, so that we serve NOT UNDER THE OLD WRITTEN CODE but in the new life of the Spirit"* (Romans 7:6). Again this had to have been addressed to Jewish believers as the gentiles had never been 'held captive' by the Law.

In the letter to the Romans, Paul explains that not only did Jesus shed His blood to pay the penalty for our sins, but He died as our representative and substitute so that, WITH RESPECT TO THE LAW, when He died, we who believe in Him died legally also. (See Romans 6:6-8). The Law exists to show us our guilt before a Holy God and our need of Atonement. The testimony of the Law to all men is that we are all guilty and in need of someone to take the wages of our sin, which is death. The testimony of our guilt, which the Law establishes, should lead us to cling to the mercy available through the sacrifice of Jesus, which was foretold and prefigured in the Hebrew Scriptures.

Paul argues, the Law has dominion over a man as long as he lives. Under the law we all stand guilty and liable to the penalty of death. Our substitute Messiah has taken the death for us and we are identified with Him in His death so that in the eyes of the law we are seen as dead. Therefore, Paul explains since we died in Christ, we "also HAVE BECOME DEAD TO THE LAW through the body of Christ;' not that we might remain lawless but that we might be *"married to another, even to Him who was raised from the dead, that we should bear fruit to God!'* (Romans 7:4)

According to Romans 7, therefore, the believer is 'DEAD TO THE LAW', and 'DISCHARGED" FROM THE LAW' The purpose of this is certainly not that we should be LAWLESS, but that we should be FREE TO OBEY AND FOLLOW JESUS.

The 'marriage' to Jesus will never be complete until we leave the Law. This is why John the Baptist calls himself 'the friend of the Bridegroom' as it is he who hands the Jewish people from the custody of the Law to the to the custody of the Bridegroom. Believers (Jew or gentile) who remain under the Law will never come to maturity and will never attain to the Bridal Company.

Should Jewish Believers Keep Some Old Testament Laws?

In the light of this, are we saying that it is wrong for Jewish believers to keep some Old Testament customs and some Jewish traditions? By no means! We are simply saying that to keep Old Testament Law *adds nothing*

- to our justification,

- to our ongoing sanctification or
- to our walk in the Spirit as obedient disciples of Jesus.

If a person wishes to rest on Saturday, abstain from shellfish, etc., he is of course free to do so, provided that he realizes that keeping such laws and customs add nothing to his redemption. Indeed many Jewish believers may want to keep some Jewish customs, traditions and parts of the Law to maintain their Jewish identity and to prevent their assimilation into the gentile culture. However, this keeping of some Jewish laws and traditions should not be construed as 'keeping the Law,' but simply as a means of identifying culturally with the Jewish people.

A New Testament, born again believer is free to keep some Jewish laws on the following conditions:

(1) that he does not believe or teach that keeping these customs advances his standing with God, his sanctification, or his walk towards perfection as a faithful disciple of Jesus;

(2) that he does not *require* others to do as he does, or imply that this makes him a superior believer than the believer who does not wish to keep these customs;

(3) that he realizes that while keeping SOME Torah laws and Jewish customs, he is aware that he is NOT UNDER THE LAW and in fact is really NOT "KEEPING THE LAW"

It is evident that an element of hypocrisy can easily creep in here. A person keeping a FEW LAWS can pretend that he is faithful to the LAW Paul accused Peter of 'playing the hypocrite' on precisely this issue.

"But when Peter came to Antioch, I withstood him to his face, because he was to be blamed; for before certain men came from James, he would eat with the gentiles; but when they came, he withdrew and separated himself, fearing those who were of the circumcision. And the rest of the Jews also played the hypocrite with him so that even Barnabas was carried away with their hypocrisy.

But when I saw that THEY WERE NOT STRAIGHTFORWARD ABOUT THE TRUTH OF THE GOSPEL, I said to Peter, before them all, "If you, being a Jew, live IN THE MANNER OF THE gentiles and not as the Jews, why do you compel gentiles to live as Jews?"' (Galatians 2:11-14)

Today some believers are tempted *to "play the hypocrite"* as Peter did until Paul corrected him. They do not really keep the Law, but they pretend to do so and require others to do so. This is not being straightforward about the gospel. If contemporary believers were serious about keeping the Law then they ought not to keep their money in an interest bearing account in a bank (even an Israeli bank!). They ought not to wear cotton underwear under their woolen sweaters etc., etc!! There are 613 laws which those under the Law are BOUND to keep. It is evident that no Jew or gentile alive today fully keeps the Law. In fact they cannot be kept today, as the Temple no longer exists.

The Ritual & Moral Laws Of Sinai

Some teach that the Sinai Laws are divided into two parts: the ceremonial and the moral laws. The believer in Jesus clearly sees that His death and resurrection have fulfilled the rituals of the temple. Some say that we are discharged from the ritual regulations of Sinai but not from the moral regulations. They fear that if we say that we are discharged from the moral regulation we will fall back into immorality and lawlessness.

Firstly it is impossible to divide the regulations of Sinai into moral and ceremonial. Some regulations are clearly moral and some are clearly ceremonial but some seem to fit neither category. E.G. is the requirement that a brother should have sexual relationship with his widowed sister-in law to give her offspring if her husband has left her without children a part of the moral law or of the ritual law? Are the dietary laws moral or ceremonial?

Paul says that we are discharged from the law: - all of them. If we have violated one of them we are as guilty as if we had violated all of them and therefore we can only establish righteousness through the channel of faith in the atoning sacrifice and grace.

Does emancipation from the law through permanent atonement give us a license to immorality? No! Because the same power that emancipates us from the Law emancipates us from the power of sin - something the law could not do (See Romans 8 1- 4) Furthermore it places a righteous heart within us (the Holy Spirit). From this new righteous heart comes all that is moral and good - the fruit of the Spirit.

Emancipation from the Law should never be thought of as emancipation from morality. This is totally against the spirit and letter of the scriptures. So while the New Covenant emancipates us from the moral and ritual restraints of the law it never condones or permits immorality but emancipates us from all immorality and sin.

As John writes the blood of Jesus cleanses us from all unrighteousness (1 John 1:9)

4

MAINTAINING JEWISH IDENTITY

As important as it is not to rely on our law keeping to establish and maintain our relationship with God it is also important for Jewish believers to maintain their Jewishness and to avoid assimilation into the non-Jewish world. Keeping some laws and customs may help towards this end.

In protecting themselves from assimilation, however, it is important that they do not attempt to re-erect the dividing wall between Jew and gentile that Jesus has broken down. God has made Jew and gentile believers one in Jesus. In keeping their identity as Jewish believers they should not lose their oneness with the entire Body of Christ. It is important that we not tear asunder what God has joined. Jewish believers in Christ should not think that they are in any way superior to their gentile brothers in Christ, and gentile believers should not think that they are superior (or inferior) to their Jewish brothers in Christ.

"For He Himself is our peace, who has made both one, and has broken down the middle wall of division between us, having abolished in His flesh the enmity that is, THE LAW OF COMMANDMENTS contained in ordinances, so as to create in Himself ONE NEW MAN FROM THE TWO thus making peace' (Ephesians 2:14-15)

It is essential that believers do not re-erect that middle wall of division between Jew and gentile. However it is also important that Jewish believers avoid assimilation. This would cause them to lose their Jewish identity and to disappear as a distinct people.[3]

---

[3] Fear of assimilation and loss of Jewish identity is one of the greatest reasons why many Jewish people resist professing faith in Jesus

Perhaps the best way for the Jewish believer to avoid assimilation is to live in Israel and speak the Hebrew language, as language and land are the keys to ethnic and cultural distinctiveness. Since both the land and the language are now restored to the Jewish people, keeping some laws and customs becomes even less necessary as a means to maintain distinctiveness. Today many Israelis make little attempt to rigorously keep the Law and yet, because of their language and their attachment to the land, they maintain their ethnic uniqueness.

What About 'Gentile' Believers Who Voluntarily Keep The Law?

In recent years there has been a desire among many non-Jewish believers to identify more closely with the Jewish people. Zechariah predicted that this would happen:

'Thus says the Lord of hosts: 'In those days ten men from every language of the nations shall grasp the sleeve of a Jewish man, saying "Let us go with

you, for we have heard that God is with you.' (Zechariah 8:23)

Some teach that non-Jewish believers who support the Jewish people ought to keep their law as a means of identifying with them (Ezek. 37)

Since our sins under the Law

- are atoned for and
- we are dead to the Law and
- the righteousness of the law is written in our heart and
- there is a change in the priesthood

Keeping the rituals of the law is not the most appropriate way to identify with the Jewish people as it undermines our witness to the sufficiency of the redemption of God in Christ. The best way for the believer from the Gentiles to identify with the Jew is NOT to pretend to be Jewish by keeping the Law but to stand with the Jewish people in helping them fulfill their distinct and irrevocable call.

This includes

- support of their restoration to the Land of Israel;
- helping them return and
- giving social assistance and support

We also should be especially supportive of our Messianic brothers and sisters working in Israel today.

We have already shown how the 'Messianic' believer is discharged and released from the Law. This applies equally to the non-Jewish believer who wishes to identify with the Jewish people. The keeping of the Law by the believer, who may consider himself to be 'Ephraim' or a restored member of the 'lost' ten tribes', is just as irrelevant to his sanctification as it is to the Jewish believer in Jesus.

However, if anyone wants to keep some of the laws (as an expression of solidarity rather than religious necessity) he may do so under the same conditions we have outlined for the Jewish believer.

The Great Commission

In His 'great commission' Jesus urged His disciples to *"Go therefore and make disciples of all nations, baptizing them in the name of the Father, the Son and of Holy Spirit, teaching them to OBSERVE ALL THINGS THAT I HAVE COMMANDED YOU; and lo, I am with you always, even to the end of the age'* (Matt. 28-19-20)

He asked His disciples (all of whom were Jews at that time) to teach all the nations to observe ALL that He had commanded them to do. If He had also commanded them to keep the Law, then it would have been necessary for those Jewish disciples to require the gentile believers to obey the Law.

We know from Acts 15 that the gentiles were NOT required to keep the Law. It follows that if the apostles obeyed Jesus' command to teach the nations to observe ALL that he had commanded THEM to do, that he had in fact NOT required obedience to the Law of them, either. He had required instead of all His disciples that they "love one another", as He had loved them. (John 13:34-35)

The Irrevocable Call & Replacement Theology

There are those who teach that the CALL OF GOD on the Jew has been forfeited and given to the Church. They argue that the Church is 'the Israel of God' that only the one who is 'circumcised in the heart' is a real Jew (See Romans 2:28). Therefore they maintain that all God's promises to the Jews have been forfeited by the Jews who have not put their faith in Jesus. It is true that there are some scriptures, WHEN TAKEN IN ISOLATION FROM THE REST OF THE NEW TESTAMENT that may give rise to such an interpretation. However (lest there be any ambiguity about the matter of God's continual call and work with the Jews who do not yet accept the Messianic claims of Jesus) the apostle Paul writes: *'For I do not desire, brethren that you should be ignorant of this mystery, lest you should be wise in your own opinion, that hardening IN PART has happened to Israel UNTIL the fullness of the gentiles has come in. And so all Israel will be saved, as it is written: "The deliverer will come out of Zion, and he will turn away ungodliness from Jacob; for this is my covenant with them, when I take away their sins!' Concerning the gospel, they are enemies for your sake, but concerning the election they are beloved for the sake of the fathers. FOR THE GIFTS AND THE CALLING OF GOD ARE IRREVOCABLE!'* (Romans 11:25-29)

Paul says here that the failure of the majority of Jews to accept the claims of Jesus has NOT caused them to forfeit their special call. God's call on them will be fulfilled. Paul gives the name "Israel" to ethnic Israelis who have resisted the claims of Jesus and does not only apply it to those that accepted Yeshua the Messiah. THE CHURCH HAS NOT REPLACED THE CALL ON THE JEWS.

> *Paul gives the name "Israel" to ethnic Israelis who have resisted the claims of Jesus and does not only apply it to those that accepted Yeshua the Messiah*

The Jewish people have a unique role to play in the drama, which God is working out, in human history.

The Church cannot replace this role. God has promised to bring them back, from all the nations, to their ancient homeland. There He will meet with them and "pour clean water upon them!"[4]

At that time the Jewish people as a whole will be grafted back into the 'Olive Tree' of God's blessings and anointings through faith in their Messiah. *"And I will pour upon the house of David, and upon the inhabitants of Jerusalem, the spirit of grace and of supplications: and they shall look upon me whom they have pierced, and they shall mourn for him, as one mourneth for his only son."* (Zecheriah 12:10) Then they will become spiritually one with those from the gentiles who through Jesus have been grafted into the Olive Tree of God's fellowship and blessing. *'Thus says the Lord God: 'Behold, 0 My people, I will open your graves and cause you to come up from your graves, and bring you into the land of Israel. 'Then you shall know that I am the Lord, ... "I will put My Spirit in you,*

---

[4] See for example Isaiah 11:11-14, Ezekiel 37: 21-22, Amos 9:14-15 Jeremiah 16:14-17, Jeremiah 31:10-12, Jeremiah 31: 27-34

and you shall live, and I will place you in your own land. Then you shall know that I, the Lord, have spoken it and performed it," says the Lord." (Ezekiel 37:12-14)

'For if you were cut out of the olive tree which is wild by nature, and were grafted contrary to nature into a good olive tree, how much more will these, who are the natural branches, be grafted into their own olive tree!' (Romans 11:24)

The sovereign hand of God is working with the Jewish people. He is gathering them back to their ancient homeland. This process will inevitably lead to their acceptance of their Messiah and to tremendous blessing on them and on the entire 'Olive Tree!' Let us be careful, in our zeal, not to pre-empt the sovereign purposes of God.

With respect to individual salvation, the Jewish people have no advantage or superiority over the gentile, but with respect to the plan of God they have a unique calling and purpose Each must pass by faith through the same 'Door! (John 10:1-9)

5

REPLACEMENT THEOLOGY

Has the Coming of Jesus fulfilled Israel's Destiny?

Some say that the coming of Jesus fulfills the call of God on the Jewish people. The promise of Abraham was that he should be blessed and through him all the families of the earth would be blessed. (Genesis 12:3) Through his descendant Jesus atonement has been made once for all for the sins of the world (Jew and Gentile) and this good news has brought God' forgiveness reconciliation and blessing to believers everywhere.

Though this is certainly true and perhaps the greatest fulfillment of the covenant God made with Abraham it does not fulfill all of the promises given to Israel nor set them aside. The promise given to

Abraham was also that he should inherit the land of Canaan, and that this was an everlasting Covenant. The Covenant promise for the Jewish people to inherit the land of promise has not been forfeited by the coming of the Messiah. Indeed the Messiah was always seen as the one who would help them to inherit their possessions.

Paul, writing after the death and resurrection of Jesus, says that God's gift and calling on the Jewish people are irrevocable (Romans 11:29).

The coming of Jesus to take away the sin of the world is not the end of all blessing of Abraham. Both Jews and Christians wait for the Messiah's triumph when He comes to establish His throne in Jerusalem. In preparation for this God has drawn His people back from all the nations in faithfulness to His covenant with Abraham to give them the land of Canaan forever (Genesis 13:15). This return of the Jewish people to their land will culminate in the retun of the Messiah and the age of redemption.

God's promise to make Abraham a blessing to all nations and to give him the land of promise is not totally fulfilled by the atoning work of Jesus and it certainly has not been set aside by the coming of Jesus as Savior. It will in fact find its highest fulfillment when He comes again as King of Israel and King of all nations.

Replacement Theology

The teaching that the church replaces Israel has been taught widely in Christian circles throughout the centuries. It has given rise to anti-Semitism and to blindness among Christians about God's purposes for the Jewish people. Happily this error is being exposed today and many Christians are repenting of wrong theology and consequent acts of injustice and even horrendous violence towards the Jews. In the future we can expect many Christians and Jews to sit together in solidarity.

There are some who have seen through the error of 'replacement theology' (the false teaching that maintains that the Church has replaced Israel) only to swing to the opposite extreme. They teach that the coming of Jesus did not REPLACE anything in the Law and the Prophets and insist on the keeping of the Laws (Torah) for Jewish believers as a matter of required obedience to God.

In their anxiety to show the compatibility and continuity between God's purposes for the Jew and for the gentile believers they present Jesus as a mere reformer of Judaism rather than as the fulfillment of all the Law and the Prophets. They are afraid that if we present Jesus as replacing anything some may get the impression that He replaced the call on Israel with the call to His disciples.

The truth: Jesus did not *replace* or revoke the call of God on the Jews (as we have seen from Romans 11) but He did *fulfill* the Old Covenant with the New Eternal Covenant in His blood. He replaced the Levitical priesthood by fulfilling it with His eternal priesthood, and the Old Law with the law of love written on the hearts of His followers. (Hebrews 8:7-13)

6
JESUS BRINGS A NEW ERA

The Word of God never changes but the Times do. Neither Jews nor Christians should be shocked with the idea of one era being replaced by another. We see this constantly throughout the history of Israel.

- The patriarchal period was replaced by the era of the Law;
- the Tabernacle in the wilderness was replaced by the Temple;
- the era of the Judges with the era of the Kings and so on. God's chosen are not frozen in a fossilized religion.

Jesus fulfilled the Law in four ways:

(1) He fulfilled the righteous demands of the Law by obeying His Father and by perfectly loving God and His neighbor.

'Jesus said to him, " *'You shall love the Lord your God with all your heart, with all your soul, and with all your mind' (Deut. 6:5) This is the first and great commandment. And the second is like it: 'You shall love your neighbor as yourself,' (Lev. 19:18) On these two commandments hang all the Law and the Prophets!" (Matt. 22:37-40)*

(2) He fulfilled it by taking on Himself the consequence and penalty of all of our disobedience to the Law; thus fulfilling the demands of the Law on us.

(3) He fulfilled the Law by fulfilling IN REALITY that which the Law anticipated IN TYPE. He became our eternal Passover Lamb; He became our eternal High Priest, thus fulfilling the priesthood and sacrifices; He became our scapegoat, fulfilling the Day of Atonement; and He poured out the Holy

Spirit on us thus fulfilling Pentecost (Shavuot) etc.

(4) The Law is fulfilled in the Messiah in the same way as the boy is fulfilled in the man, the caterpillar in the butterfly, the bud in the blossom. The boyhood stage is a stage on the way to maturity; the bud is a stage on the way to the blossom. The mature cannot remain within the confines of the bud

The Curse Of The Law

All men (Jew and Gentile) remain under the law until we accept and put our faith in the finished work of Messiah Jesus on the Cross. Until then the testimony of guilt of the Law remains as a dreadful testimony of guilt over the lives of all. So Hebrews does not say that the law *is* obsolete but that it is *becoming* obsolete. It remains forever but becomes obsolete over our lives only as we enter the Kingdom of God.

This testimony of guilt makes it impossible to enjoy the blessings of God's abundance promised in Deuteronomy 28 and throughout the Bible. The release from the guilt-testimony curse of Law through the atoning sacrifice of Messiah Jesus now makes it possible for all believers to enjoy the abundance of God's blessings and promises. *"Christ hath **redeemed** us from the curse of the law, being made a curse for us: for it is written, 'Cursed is every one that hangeth on a tree', that the blessing of Abraham might come on the Gentiles through Jesus Christ; that we might receive the promise of the Spirit through faith."* (Galatians 3:13 - 14))

The Era Of The Law is Temporary But The Word of God is forever

When we say that the era of the Sinai Law is temporary we are not saying that the Word of God in the Hebrew Scriptures is temporary. *"The grass withers, the flower fades, but the word of God shall stand forever."* (Isaiah 40.8)

A problem arises from the different words that are used. The Hebrew word "Torah" means "Law"; the words "Dabar Elohim" mean "Word of God" and the word "Tanach" means "The Law, The Prophets & The Writings". These terms can cause confusion. Traditionally Jewish people refer to the "Word of God" as the "Torah" (Law) rather than the "Dabar Elohim" (Word of God) or "Tanach."

The Word of God endures forever, but the era of Israel's restraint under the religious law of Sinai was, (according to the Hebrew Scriptures themselves) temporary. To move beyond the jurisdiction and elementary principles of the Law, should never be construed as abandoning the Hebrew Scriptures with their eternal promises, prophecies and standards. They are the basis of the New Testament and are used in about 1600 New Testament Scriptures. The move from the external restraints of the Law to the inner restraints of the New Covenant is not an abandonment of the Word of God, but a fulfillment of what that Word foretold.

A similar problem has arisen among New Testament believers who move beyond the letter of the Law to the law of the Spirit of life and a life

> *To move beyond the jurisdiction and elementary principles of the Torah should never be construed as abandoning the Hebrew Scriptures with their eternal promises, prophecies and righteous standards*

governed by the fruit of the Spirit rather than by external ordinances. In declaring themselves "not under the Law" they sometimes assume that the Hebrew scriptures do not apply to today. They confuse emancipation from the guilt and penalty of the Law through the death of Jesus to emancipation from the Word of God.

The Law is not the enemy of the gospel, for through it came the knowledge of sin and of our need of a savior (Romans 3:20), but it was powerless to make anyone righteous. It restrained us UNTIL Christ came. (Gal. 3:23) It was our custodian UNTIL Christ should come. (Gal. 3:24) It was added because of transgressions, UNTIL the offspring should come. (Galatians 3:19) Jesus said: *'The law and the prophets were UNTIL John the Baptist since then the kingdom of God is preached!'* (Luke 16:16) The whole era of the Law was intended by God to be temporary. The Letter to the Hebrews says that the Law is now becoming 'obsolete!' (Hebrews 8:13), but the Word of God 'dabar Elohim' or 'Torah' as it is often called, endures forever

It is clear from this frequent use of the word "UNTIL" in reference to the law that God did not intend for the Sinai Laws to rule over his people forever. The word 'until' is the same word as used by Jesus in Luke 21:24 when he refers to the times of the gentiles.

'Jerusalem will be trodden down by the gentiles until the times of the gentiles are fulfilled' In other words, He foretold that the gentile nations would not dominate Jerusalem forever, but only for a certain period of time. The word 'until' is the same word as is used in Acts 3:21 concerning the temporary physical absence of Jesus from this earth. *'Jesus, whom heaven must receive until the times of restoration of all things!'* The word 'until' means temporary, not forever.

The jurisdiction of the Law is over for all who come to Christ but the call of God on the Jewish people, which preceded the law, is ***irrevocable***, and has ***not*** been replaced. The Law is still needed to bear witness to our sinfulness and our need of Atonement. That is why Hebrews does not say that the law is *'obsolete'* but that it *'is becoming obsolete.'* (Hebrews 8:13 for those who believe on the Atoning Sacrifice of Jesus)

Beware Of The Leaven Of The Pharisees

In the course of His earthly ministry there are only two groups of people that incurred the wrath of Jesus. Each has their counterparts in the Church of today. It is distressing to the Spirit of Jesus to see the spirit and teaching of the Pharisees enter into the believers. In Matthew chapter 16, Jesus warns His disciples to *"beware of the leaven of the Pharisees and Sadducees."* (Mt 16:11) The leaven of the Pharisees Matthew explains is the teaching of the Pharisees.

Many of the Pharisees later believed and came to faith in Jesus. Some of them wanted to require the gentile believers to be circumcised. *"But some believers, who belonged to the party of the Pharisees rose up, and said, "It is necessary to circumcise them and to charge them to keep the*

Law of Moses." (Acts 15:5) They did not win their case at the Council of Jerusalem, but they remained a strong influence on the church in Jerusalem.

Sadly, the teaching of the Pharisees is returning among some believers in our day. The Holy Spirit warns against this.

Dear reader, do not throw away your liberty in Christ; stand in it; stand in the grace to which He has brought you, and live in the NEW LIFE OF LOVE through the presence of Christ's Spirit in you. Stand in solidarity with the Jewish people as the scripture commands but do not get entangled with the teachings of the "Pharisees".

7

OBJECTIONS & REFUTATIONS

A few more matters need to be squarely addressed before we conclude this study. As we noted there are some scriptures in the New Testament, which if out of context may lead some to conclude that we should keep the Law, or that Jewish believers, in Jesus should keep the Law. There are those who would advance the following passages as objections:

Objection (1)

Jesus said: *"Do not think that I came to destroy (kataluoo) the Law or the Prophets. I did not come to destroy, but to fulfill (pleremoo). For assuredly I say to you, till heaven and earth pass away, one jot or one tittle will by no means pass from the law till all is fulfilled. Whoever therefore breaks one of the least of these commandments, and teaches men so, shall be called least in the kingdom of heaven; but whoever does and teaches them, he shall be called great in the kingdom of heaven.'* (Mt. 5:17-19) Some will object that from this passage Jesus teaches that we should keep all the Laws of Sinai

Refutation (1)

Jesus says here that he came not to destroy the law and the prophets but to fulfill them. Everything in the law and the prophets *will* be fulfilled.

In Luke's Gospel 24:27, Jesus explains how He had fulfilled the Law and the prophets: "*And beginning at Moses and all the Prophets he explained to them in all the scriptures concerning himself.*" He showed how He had fulfilled the Law and the Prophets in His entire ministry and work.

He then asks His disciples to keep HIS TEACHINGS (John 14:23) NOT the Law If He had been asking us to keep the Law, then the apostle Paul would have been a false teacher when he said that we are *'discharged from the Law'* (Romans 7:6). All the apostles would have been false teachers too in not requiring or teaching that the gentile believers should keep the Law. (See also remarks made earlier about The Great Commission.)

The teachings that Jesus asks us to keep are *His* teachings. These teachings demand love towards God and our neighbor and they produce a deeper righteousness than that asked by the Law and the Pharisees and Scribes. With Him the **inner attitudes** must be right. Not only is adultery forbidden but the root of adultery, which is lust, must be dealt with. Not only is murder forbidden, but also the vengeful anger, which is the seed of murder, must be dealt with. *'Jesus said: It is not what goes into the mouth defiles a man; but what comes out of the mouth, this defiles a man'* (Mt. 15:11); See also Peter's vision in Acts 10:15)

No Christian can make the excuse of saying: 'I am justified by faith, so it matters not how I behave' for Jesus demands[5] of us a pure heart and pure behavior if we are to enter the kingdom. Paul reiterates (this point in the 5th chapter of Galatians.)

The teachings Jesus asks us to keep are *his teachings*. He who breaks any one of *these* teachings will be called least in the kingdom of heaven. The word 'these' refers to His teachings which He is expositing in the Sermon on the Mount. It is in the context of the Sermon on the Mount that we have His reference to fulfilling the Law and teaching 'these' teachings. If He had been referring to the Law then we would have to say that all the heroes of the church from Peter and Paul, to St. Francis, John Wesley, Charles Spurgeon to Corrie Ten Boom, are least in the kingdom of heaven, because they did not keep the Jewish Law. We regard them as heroes of the faith, however, because they are examples to us of the law of love.

---

[5] With the demand there is also an impartation of a new pure heart though the Holy Spirit which enables us to keep His requirement

Jesus did not destroy the Law. The Law remains unchanged. BUT WE WHO BELIEVE HAVE CHANGED. We have become dead to the law and are discharged from it to serve now in the newness of the spirit.

The word to 'keep' (as in 'keep the law') is 'tereo' Jesus could have easily said: 'I came not to destroy the Law, but to keep it: but He did not say that, but said that He came to fulfill it. Not once did He ask His disciples to KEEP the Law, but he DID frequently ask them to keep (tereo) His commands works and teachings.

'If you love me, keep my commandments:' (John 14:15) "He who has my commandments and keeps them it is he who loves me. And he who loves me will be loved by My Father, and I will love him and manifest myself to him:' (John 14:21)

"If anyone loves Me he will KEEP MY WORDS and My Father will love him and we will come to him and make our home with Him. (John 14:23) "If you keep My commandments you will abide in My love,

just as I have kept my Father's commandment and abide in His love." (John 15:10)

In none of these references does He ask us to keep His commandments AND the Law, but He simply asks us to keep HIS COMMANDMENTS.

Objection (2) The Rich Young Man

Jesus said to a certain rich young man that came to Him: *'If you want to enter into life, keep the commandments: "He said to Him, 'Which ones?' Jesus said "'You shall not murder, You shall not steal, You shall not bear false witness, Honor your father and your mother, and You shall love your neighbor as yourself,' "The young man said to Him, "All these things I have kept from my youth. What do I still lack?" Jesus said to him "If you want to be perfect, go sell what you have and give to the poor, and you will have treasure in heaven; and come follow Me" '* (Mt. 19:17-21) Some regard this passage as a reference that Jesus followers should adhere strictly to the Law

Refutation (2)

It is worth noting that of the 613 laws of the Old Covenant Jesus only demanded six of them of the rich young man. These six are all covered by Jesus' new commandment, *'Love one another as I have loved you.'*

The young man still lacked something and Jesus went on to point out to him that the way to perfection and wholeness was to follow HIM. This exchange, far from reinforcing the position that Jesus requires some to keep the Law, serves only to show that Jesus was aware that the 'law made nothing perfect' and completeness could only be attained by going further than the law through the commandments of Jesus.

Objection (3)

Paul says: *'we establish the law' and* in Romans 3:31 he writes*: 'Do we then make void the law through faith? Certainly not! On the contrary, we establish the law!'* (Romans 3:31) Therefore, it is argued, believers should adhere to the Law

Refutation (3)

Paul is arguing with those who say that his message of justification through faith rather than by works of the law is foreign to the teaching in the Law. He goes on to show that the Law (the Torah) teaches that Abraham was justified by faith, and that the principle of imputed righteousness apart from the works of the Law is revealed in the Hebrew Scriptures also. He quotes Psalm 32:1-2: *"Blessed are those whose lawless deeds are forgiven, And whose sins are covered. Blessed is the man to whom the Lord shall not impute sin."*

The way of justification ***by faith*** is revealed throughout the Law and the Prophets. Indeed he goes on to point out that it is the only way to justification. *'By deeds of the law no flesh will be justified!'* (Romans 3:20) He says that the righteousness of God apart from the Law is now revealed but it is 'witnessed to by' the Law and the Prophets. Paul's teaching is that the Law was added because of transgression. It never made anyone righteous; but the message of the law and the prophets themselves is that righteousness is attained ***not*** by works of the Law but by forgiveness and faith. His teaching is witnessed to by the Law and is not in contradiction to the teachings of the Torah.

The law of love fulfills the righteousness, which the Law could not produce.

'Owe no one anything except to love one another, for he who loves another has fulfilled the law. For the commandments, "You shall not commit adultery;' "You shall not murder;' "You shall not steal;' "You shall not bear false witness;' "You shall not covet;' AND IF THERE IS ANY OTHER COMMANDMENT are ALL summed up in this saying, namely, "You shall love your neighbor as yourself." Love does not harm to a neighbor; therefore LOVE IS THE FULFILLMENT OF THE LAW' (Romans 13:8-10)

The 'law of Christ' (see Galatians 6:2) is fulfilled not through Torah observance but by being filled with the love of God, through the Holy Spirit and expressing that love towards others.

"For all the law is fulfilled in one word, even in this: 'You shall love your neighbor as yourself.": (Galatians 5:4) *"Bear one another's burdens, and so fulfill the Law of Christ."* (Galatians 6:2)

We are not attempting to void the Law but to establish what it points to. Moses himself said: *'The Lord your God will raise up for you a Prophet like me from your midst from your brethren. HIM YOU SHALL HEAR..'* (Deut. 18:15) Peter in reference to Jesus in Acts (3:22) quotes this passage. Moses himself points to another prophetic lawgiver who would come after him. At Jesus' baptism and at His transfiguration, God the Father's voice was heard urging the hearers to FOLLOW JESUS. He bore witness to the fact that Jesus was to be obeyed and that following Him eclipsed the ministry of John the Baptist and Moses.

From the day of Jesus' baptism, John, (a figure of the Law and the prophets) had to decrease as Jesus increased. On the Mount of the Transfiguration when Peter wanted to make three booths one for Moses (the representative of the

Law) one for Elijah and one for Jesus. The voice of the Father was heard saying: *'This is my beloved Son, in whom I am well pleased.'* HEAR HIM!" Peter wanted to obey Moses and Jesus; but Moses was destined, like John, to decrease that Jesus the Light of the world could be seen. *'Looking up they saw only Jesus.'* The light of Moses and Elijah was fading. (See Mt. 17)

Objection (4)

When Paul went to Jerusalem the Believers there claimed to be 'zealous for the Law:' therefore zeal for the law is the norm for New Testament believers.

Refutation

It is true that when Paul went to Jerusalem some believers there claimed to be *'zealous for the law'* and while in Jerusalem Paul submitted to the rituals of purification prescribed under the Old Law. (See Acts 21) Does any reader of the New Testament really believe that Paul was out of right fellowship with God, when God was mightily using him among the gentiles, with miracles flowing through his ministry?

According to the Law Paul was ritually unclean during that time, but obviously he was not out of fellowship with God. This proves more than ever that our ritual cleanness according to the Law has nothing to do with right standing with God since the shedding of the Blood of Jesus, atones for our sins and purifies us from all uncleanness. *"But if we walk in the light, as he is in the light, we have fellowship one with another, and the **blood of Jesus** Christ his Son cleanseth us from all sin.."* (1 John 1:7)

The prophet Agabus had warned Paul that if he went up to Jerusalem he would be put into bondage by the people in Jerusalem. He counted the cost of going into bondage for the sake of the goal of His mission to witness in Jerusalem and in Rome. It is possible that he foresaw arrest in Jerusalem as a means to getting to Rome which it proved to be.

The fact that Paul submitted to the ritual does not imply that he put any value on it apart from an opportunity to go along with the customs of the people so that they would permit him to speak to them. If he, who taught that one could eat meat sacrificed to idols provided that it did not violate one's conscience, was free to eat such meat, surely he would have felt free to undergo the ritual of purification. No endorsement of the practice is implied. There is no reason to take Paul's submission to the rituals imposed on him in Jerusalem as meaning anything more than that he did not want to cause offense. It is notable how silent he is when those zealous for the Law are requiring him to be purified.

When Paul finally does speak up in Acts 22 it is to recount once again his conversion. He says to the Jews that *before* his encounter with Jesus on the road to Damascus he too had been 'zealous for the Law'. He points out that this zeal only made him hostile to Christ and led him to persecute Jesus' followers. His zeal for the Law is now replaced by a zeal for the gospel. *'I am indeed a Jew, born in Tarsus of Cilicia, but brought up in this city at the feet of Gamaliel, taught according to the strictness of our father's law, and WAS zealous toward God as you all are today. I persecuted this Way.'* (Acts 22:3-4)

It is true that in Acts 21 the elders 'who were with James' claimed to be zealous for the Law; but Peter in Acts 15 admits that they all failed to keep the law. *"Now therefore, why do you test God by putting a yoke on the neck of the disciples which **neither our fathers nor we were able to bear**? But we believe that through the grace of the Lord Jesus Christ we shall be **saved in the same manner as they**"* (Acts 15:11) There is no other way of being saved, staying saved and progressing in grace for Jew or gentile.

8

CONCLUSION

This study is written out of deepest concern for many of God's children, who have tasted His salvation through grace and now are seeking to return to the Law as a pathway for obedience and holiness.

Jesus has not left us without law; He has brought a new law, which we fulfill when we walk in love. James tells us not to judge one another according to the *Law 'for whoever shall keep the whole law, and yet stumble in one point he is guilty of all.'* (James 2:10) It is evident that under the law we all stand permanently guilty. But in Christ we stand eternally acquitted provided we continue in

Him and walk in love and obedience to His teachings and to His ways.

The book of Hebrews teaches that we believers (from BOTH Jewish and Gentile backgrounds) have NOT come to Mount Sinai i.e. the realm of the Law but *to "Mount Zion and to the city of the living God, the heavenly Jerusalem, to an innumerable company of angels .... and to JESUS THE MEDIATOR OF THE NEW COVENANT, AND TO THE BLOOD OF SPRINKLING that speaks better things than that of Abel"* (Hebrews 12:18-24)

Today God is calling His people to make the journey from Sinai to Zion - from the realm of the Law to the realm of the New Covenant and of the Holy Spirit. For it was on Zion that Jesus mediated a New Covenant at His Last Supper and it was here also that the Holy Spirit was poured out.

> *Today God is calling His people to make the journey from Sinai to Zion - from the realm of the Law to the realm of the New Covenant and of the Holy Spirit.*

'No one can serve two masters; for either he will hate the one and love the other, or else he will be loyal to the one and despise the other' (Mt. 6:24)

This principle of Jesus applies to the question of serving God under the Law or in the Spirit. To serve under the Law is to receive constant condemnation; to serve in the Spirit is to be released to love. To go back under the Law is to go into the flesh; to live in the Spirit enables us to walk in love. The New Covenant (as we have seen) gives no license to sin because it liberates us from sin's power and empowers us to live an upright love by the power and impartation of the Spirit.

Believer, Christ died for you and reconciled you to God, if He died for you and won your redemption, and set you free of all that you could not be freed from under Moses, follow Him, and walk in love. Jesus says to you today "Come, Follow Me!" THERE IS NO OTHER WAY

APPENDIX
LET THE SCRIPTURES SPEAK!

'F or whoever shall keep the whole law, and yet stumble in one point, he is guilty of all.' (James 1:10)

'For as many as are of the works of the law are under the curse; for it is written, "Cursed is everyone who does not continue in all things which are written in the book of the law, to do them. But that no one is justified by the law in the sight of God is evident, for "the just shall live by faith." Yet the law is not of faith, but, 'The man who does them shall live by them.' Christ has redeemed us from the curse of the law, having become a curse for us (for it is written, "Cursed is everyone who hangs upon a tree"), that the blessing of Abraham might come upon the gentiles in Christ Jesus, that we might

receive the promise of the Spirit through faith.' (Galatians 3:10-14)

'What purpose then does the law serve? It was added because of transgressions, TILL the Seed should come to whom the promise was made.': (Galatians 3:19)

'But before faith came, we were kept under guard by the law, kept for the faith which would afterward be revealed. Therefore the law was our tutor to bring us to Christ, that we might be justified by faith. But after faith has come, we are NO LONGER under a tutor. For you are all sons of God through faith in Christ Jesus.' (Galatians 3:23-25)

'But now AFTER your have known God, or rather are known by God, how is it that you turn again to the weak and beggarly elements to which you desire again to be in bondage? You observe days and months and seasons and years. I am afraid for you, lest I have labored for you in vain.' (Galatians 4:9-11)

'Therefore, if you died with Christ from the basic principles of the world, why as though living in the world, do you subject yourselves to regulations — "Do not touch, do not taste, do not handle;' which all concern things which perish with the using — according to the commandments and doctrines of men? These things have an appearance of wisdom and self-imposed religion, false humility, and neglect of the body, but are of no value against the indulgence of the flesh:' (Colossians 2:20-23)

'For on the one hand there is an annulling of the former commandment because of its weakness and unprofitableness, for the law made nothing perfect; on the other hand, there is the bringing in of a better hope, through which we draw near to God:.' (Hebrews 7:18-19)

"Therefore, if perfection were through the Levitical priesthood (for under it the people received the law), what further need was there that another priest should rise according to the order of Melchizedek, and not be called according to the

order of Aaron? For the priesthood being changed, of necessity there is also a change of the law." (Hebrews 7:11-12)

'For if that first covenant had been faultless, then no place would have been sought for a second.' (Hebrews 8:7)

'For the law, having a shadow of the good things to come, and not the very image of the things can never with these same sacrifices which they offer continually year by year, make those who approach perfect.' (Hebrews 10:1)

'For you have not come to the mountain that may be touched and that burned with fire; (i.e. Mt. Sinai where the Law was given).. *'But you have come to Mount Zion and the city of the living God, the heavenly Jerusalem, to an innumerable company of angels, to the general assembly and church of the firstborn.'* (Hebrews 12:18 - 23)

'For sin shall not have dominion over you, for you are not under law but under grace.' (Romans 6:14)

"And having been set free from sin, you became slaves of righteousness."(Romans 6:18)

"Therefore my brethren you also have become dead to the law through the body of Christ, that you may be married to another, even to Him who was raised from the dead, that we should bear fruit for God. For when we were in the flesh, the passions of sins, which were aroused by the law, were at work in our members to bear fruit to death. But now we have been delivered from the law, having died to what we were held by, so that we should serve in the newness of the Spirit and not on the oldness of the letter" (Romans 7:4-6)

'For I through the law died to the law that I might live to God. I have been crucified with Christ; it is no longer I who live, but Christ lives in me and the life which I now live in the flesh I live by faith in the Son of God, who loved me and gave Himself for me. I do not set aside the grace of God for if righteousness comes through the law, then Christ died in vain.' (Gal. 2:19-21)

'For freedom Christ has made us free; stand fast therefore in the liberty by which Christ has made us free, and do not be entangled again with a yoke of bondage:' Indeed I, Paul, say to you that if you become circumcised, Christ will profit you nothing. And I testify again to every man who becomes circumcised that he is a debtor to keep the whole law. You have become estranged from Christ, you who attempt to be justified by law; you have fallen from grace.' (Galatians 5:1-4)

'Owe no one anything except to love one another, for he who loves another has fulfilled the law. For the commandments, "You shall not commit adultery;' "You shall not murder," "You shall not steal;' "You shall not bear false witness." "You shall not covet;' and if there is any other commandment are all summed up in this saying, namely, "You shall love your neighbor as yourself." Love does no harm to a neighbor; therefore LOVE IS THE FULFILLMENT OF THE LAW.' (Romans 13:8-10)

'For all the law is fulfilled in one word, even in this: "You shall love your neighbor as yourself."' (Galatians 5:14)

'But the fruit of the Spirit is love, joy, peace, longsuffering, kindness, goodness, faithfulness, gentleness, self-control. Against such there is no law.' (Galatians 5:22-23)

'You search the Scriptures, for in them you think you have eternal life; and these are they which testify of Me. But you are not willing to come to Me that you may have life!' (John 5:39-40)

'If anyone thirsts, let him come to Me and drink.' (John 7:37)

'I am the way, the truth, and the life. No one comes to the Father except through Me.' (Jn 14:6)

'In speaking of a new covenant He treats the first as obsolete. And what is becoming obsolete and growing old is ready to vanish away.' (Hebrews 8:13)

PRAYER TO ACCEPT GOD'S ATONEMENT

O God of my Fathers I thank You that you have provided atonement for my sins - an innocent victim to take on himself all my past and present sins. I thank You for giving me the Law that shows me that I am a sinner in need of your mercy.

I turn to You and accept the provision of the blood of Jesus you have given to take away my sins

I lay on the scapegoat Yeshua all my sins and the sinful part of my nature and I ask that the Holy Spirit of God - the Spirit of Yeshua will fill my heart. I believe that Yeshua who died for my sins and rose again for my justification is my atoning sacrifice and I ask His Spirit into my heart to give me a new heart and the Spirit of God's righteousness and love,

I am born from above because my sins are forgiven and God's spirit dwells in me.

Thank you God My Father for providing atonement and thank you Yeshua for going to such humiliation to be my scapegoat. Amen

ABOUT THE AUTHORS

Paul & Nuala O'Higgins are the directors of Reconciliation Outreach. They are natives of Ireland now living in Stuart, Florida. They travel extensively in an international ministry of teaching and reconciliation. They are dedicated to worldwide interdenominational evangelism. Paul holds a doctorate in Biblical theology. They are the authors of several books and are called to be part of the movement to renew restore and prepare the church end of age.

OTHER BOOKS BY PAUL & NUALA O'HIGGINS

- **Christianity Without Religion**
- **In Israel Today With Jesus**
- **The Double Gift Of The Holy Spirit**
- **The Tree Of Life**

THE ONE NEW MAN SERIES

Vol 1   The Four Great Covenants
Vol 2   New Testament Believer's & The Law
Vol 3   The Feasts Of The Lord
Vol 4   The Regathering Of Israel & The Climax Of History

For more copies of these books and for more copies of **"New Testament Believers & The Law"** write:

Reconciliation Outreach
P.O. Box 2778, Stuart, FL 34995
Or call 772-283-6920 Or 1-800 258-5416
and send donation to cover cost of book plus shipping.